CANTORA

Mercedes Sosa, The Voice of Latin America

For those who raise their voice

THIS IS A BORZOI BOOK PUBLISHED BY ALFRED A. KNOPF

Copyright © 2023 by Melisa Fernández Nitsche

All rights reserved. Published in the United States by Alfred A. Knopf, an imprint of Random House Children's Books, a division of Penguin Random House LLC, New York.

Knopf, Borzoi Books, and the colophon are registered trademarks of Penguin Random House LLC.

Visit us on the Web! rhcbooks.com

Educators and librarians, for a variety of teaching tools, visit us at RHTeachersLibrarians.com

Library of Congress Cataloging-in-Publication Data
Names: Fernández Nitsche, Melisa, author.
Title: Cantora : Mercedes Sosa, the voice of Latin America / Melisa Fernández Nitsche.
Description: First edition. | New York : Alfred A. Knopf Books for Young Readers, 2023. | Audience: Ages 4–8 |
Audience: Grades 2–3 | Summary: "A picture book about the Latin American folk singer Mercedes Sosa.
Mercedes performed the world over, sharing stories through song."—Provided by publisher
Identifiers: LCCN 2022052477 (print) | LCCN 2022052478 (ebook) | ISBN 978-0-593-64597-0 (hardcover) |
ISBN 978-0-593-64598-7 (library binding) | ISBN 978-0-593-64599-4 (ebook)
Subjects: LCSH: Sosa, Mercedes—Juvenile literature. | Singers—Argentina—Biography—Juvenile literature. |
LCGFT: Biographies. | Picture books. Classification: LCC ML3930.S686 N57 2023 (print) |
LCC ML3930.S686 (ebook) | DDC 782.4216492 [B]—dc23/eng/20221103

The text of this book is set in 13-point Amasis.
The illustrations were created using Procreate.
Book design by Sarah Hokanson

MANUFACTURED IN CHINA
10 9 8 7 6 5 4 3 2 1   First Edition

CANTORA

MERCEDES SOSA, THE VOICE OF LATIN AMERICA

MELISA FERNÁNDEZ NITSCHE

Alfred A. Knopf · New York

What if a voice became a symbol of justice?
I'm here to offer my heart, said that voice.

The voice of Mercedes Sosa.

Mercedes grew up in San Miguel de Tucumán, Argentina. A place where valleys are vibrant and the high peaks of the mountains reach the sky.

She loved the sweet scent of the orange trees and the buzzing sound of the cicadas, which announced the arrival of warmer days.

Mercedes played in the park with her brothers, their beating hearts flying free.

She'd hear songs on the neighbors' radio and shyly hum along under her breath.

Back home, Mercedes's mother cooked for the whole family. Her hands made magic with just a few ingredients. The salty, rich taste of her homemade locro would soothe some of the hardships of poverty.

Mercedes's father worked in the sugar factory, and her mother washed and ironed clothes.

She saw how hard her parents worked and how little money they got.

It didn't seem fair.

One morning at school, the principal asked Mercedes to stand and sing the national anthem.

"Sing loudly, Mercedes!" she said. "Sing loudly, and we'll follow you."

Although Mercedes was embarrassed, she sang.

LIBERTAD

LIBERTAD

2A

LIBERTAD

Her voice left the students
and teachers in awe.

That same day, her friends convinced her to sing in a radio competition.

"Name?" asked the announcer.

"Gladys Osorio," she mumbled, making up a new name for herself.

When she finished her song, the announcer declared the contest over.

"Even if a thousand participants show up, no one will sing like you, Gladys," he told her.

From then on, Mercedes never stopped singing.

She used her real name when performing, but was still nervous and looked down at the stage.

After a few songs, she built up the courage to peer at the people in the audience.

Her honest, loving gaze captured the hearts of everyone listening.

With a bombo by her side, Mercedes didn't feel so shy anymore.
The instrument beat and BEAT along with her voice. The sound
echoed with the words. It became a compass for her music.

I WANT
BOOM

Mercedes sang with her soul.

Her voice gave life to the folk lyrics she chose to sing. Stories about children living in the streets, tired farmers, and the unfair pay of workers like her mother and father.

Stories much like hers.

People started calling her "the voice of the voiceless." She made it her mission to tell their stories. Mercedes wasn't just a singer anymore. She was a *cantora*.

"Anyone can sing," she said. "I'm a cantora because singing is my duty."

Mercedes's voice knew no boundaries.

She became a bridge between cultures, languages, and generations.

She took these stories to every corner of the world,
making Latin folk music popular and mixing it with pop,
rock, and tango.

But not everyone in Argentina wanted her to speak up. The military dictatorship threatened Mercedes and banned her records.

"Her songs are too powerful," they said. "People are protesting against us through her music."

Mercedes's heart trembled and raced through each performance.

The threats should have stopped her, but she kept on singing.

THEY NEED MY HEART! she shouted.

Until she was arrested in the middle of a show.

After spending all night imprisoned, Mercedes was freed.

She had to flee to Europe, carrying only her bombo, three suitcases, and a handbag.

But some things didn't fit in her luggage. . . .

Mercedes missed her family.

She'd hear Spanish songs
on the radio and hum along
under her breath.

In exile, she couldn't taste her mother's homemade locro,

and the sweet scent of the orange trees was nowhere to be found.

The love for her homeland only grew stronger.

The farther you are from home, the closer it is to your heart, she thought.

Three years in exile felt endless to Mercedes. She longed to go back to Argentina. The minutes felt like hours, and the hours like days, until at last . . .

. . . she could finally go home.

Mercedes was afraid she had been forgotten. But children, farmers, and workers welcomed her by singing her songs, while gauchos on horseback escorted her home.

Mercedes was back in her homeland, singing
louder than ever, her heart flying free.

Mercedes's voice still beats strongly today, just like her bombo did.
A voice committed to telling stories about Latin America.
A voice so powerful it became a symbol of justice.
The voice of a cantora, who was here to offer her heart.